AF323371

Caribbean

The Caribbean is a large sea almost entirely surrounded by land. Central America and part of South America form its borders to the west and south, while its northern and eastern boundaries are marked by two groups of islands – the Greater Antilles and the Lesser Antilles.

The islands were discovered by Christopher Columbus in 1492. Since then, the islanders (whom Columbus mistakenly called "Indians") have seen the influx of many other nationalities – Spanish, British, French, Dutch, and Danish colonists, slaves brought from Africa to work on the Europeans' sugar plantations, and immigrants from India. The U.S. has also exerted a strong influence in the region and, most recently, the economies of some of the islands have come to rely heavily on foreign tourists. These factors have left their mark and today the Caribbean is a melting pot of cultures.

In *We live in the Caribbean* a cross section of people, young and old, men and women, tell you what life is like in the Caribbean islands – life in the cities and in the countryside, in the mountains and by the sea.

John Griffiths is a lecturer, author and photographer specializing in the Caribbean and Latin America. He has traveled extensively to collect these twenty-six accounts of life in Jamaica, Puerto Rico, Trinidad, Tobago, Barbados, Antigua, St. Kitts, Cuba, Haiti, and the Dominican Republic.

USA
Havana
Matanzas
Trinidad
CUBA
JAMAICA
Kingston
Cap-Haitien
HAITI
Port-au-Prince
DOMINICAN REPUBLIC
Santo Domingo
San Juan
PUERTO RICO
Fajardo
TORTOLA
St. BARTHELEMY
BARBUDA
St. KITTS
NEVIS
ANTIGUA
CARIBBEAN SEA
Bridgetown
BARBADOS
TOBAGO
Port of Spain
TRINIDAD
PANAMA
COLOMBIA
VENEZUELA
GUYANA
BRAZIL

we live in the
CARIBBEAN

John Griffiths

The Bookwright Press
New York · 1985

Living Here

The author and publishers would like to acknowledge with thanks the kind help of BWIA International Airways who provided the author with free transport around the Caribbean.

First published in the United States in 1985 by
The Bookwright Press, 387 Park Avenue South,
New York NY 100126

First published in 1984 by
Wayland (Publishers) Ltd
49 Lansdowne Place, Hove
East Sussex BN3 1HF, England

Library of Congress Catalog Card Number: 84–72050
Printed in Italy by G. Canale & C.S.p.A., Turin

Contents

"Flying fish is our speciality"

Winifred Gittens works at Oistins Fish Market at Ash Bay, Barbados. The fish — dolphin, kingfish and flying fish — is bought from the local fishermen, cleaned and sold in the market.

There are more women than men working in this fish market — thirty-six women and just one man! The fishermen go out and catch the fish and when they bring in the catch, usually late in the afternoon, we buy it from them to sell in the market.

We work here six days a week from twelve noon to nine at night. When those boats come in everybody wants the fish. We sell whatever they bring in — dolphin, kingfish, flying fish. Flying fish is our speciality. We gut them and then take out all the bones and sell them ten at a time. It's a very sweet fish and the people want to eat it all the time, especially since we've done all the messy work for them.

We earn a living wage from our work, but no more than that. The price of fish has fallen because more and more fishermen are going to sea. Fish used to be cheap in Barbados only from April on, but now it is cheap from December. The price of

The fish are gutted and filleted before they are sold in the market.

A small fishing boat sets out from Oistins, Barbados.

fish is so low that the fishermen find it hard to make ends meet. But there's no other work for them; they can't go off and cut cane. I don't know how some of them will pay for their boats. Already there is a lot of tension and argument among the fishermen. Perhaps the government will step in and buy some of the fish for canning and export it. That would help us all.

Fishing is a difficult and dangerous job. The weather can change without warning and the little boats can't sail in very rough seas. The big boats that carry ice on board can sail as far as Trinidad but the smaller boats have to stay closer to shore. If they didn't their catch would spoil before they brought it in.

All the women working here have families and many of us have to bring up our children on our own. But today life is much better for us than it used to be. We've got better housing and we eat better, too. For our children, though, the changes are nothing short of miraculous. All our children now have an education, and they can even go to college. There were always bright children, but they used to have no chance of an education. Now they study and get good jobs in the government or even go abroad to work. None of them want to earn their living in the fish market or by going to sea, and we have to be pleased about that.

"Cutting field after field of cane"

Hector Ramos, 47, is a *machetero*, or sugarcane cutter from the town of Trinidad in Cuba. Although more than half of Cuba's cane is now cut by machines, Hector still works in the traditional way — with a machete.

Sugar may taste sweet but if there is a harder job than cutting the sugarcane, I don't know what it is. When I was a child I was aware of the harshness of the work but I had no idea what it meant until I became a *machetero*, a cane cutter, myself.

Hector still cuts sugarcane in the traditional way – with a machete.

When the *zafra*, or harvest, is on we cut cane from the time the sun comes up until it goes down. In this climate, in this heat, it takes all my energy to do the work, swinging the machete, cutting field after field of cane. Perhaps I am one of the last of the *macheteros* in Cuba. Already more than 50 percent of our cane is cut by machines, huge *combinatos* that cut the

When Hector has cut the cane, it is taken from the field in bullock carts.

cane out of the ground. But they can only operate in perfectly flat fields; in all the others, even where there is only a gentle slope, the human element is needed.

In the past, cane cutters only worked during the *zafra* and had no work and no wages for the rest of the year, the "Dead Season," as we called it. Life is better for us now; we work all year and, what is more, our skills have been recognized. A beginner can't just pick up a machete and start cutting cane efficiently. *Macheteros* like me can cut a lot of cane because we are experienced, and now we get well paid for our work.

It is good to know that the importance of our work is recognized, because sugar is still the most significant part of our economy and it looks as if it will be for a long time to come. For us, the problem is that we have no control over the price we get for our sugar – that's decided elsewhere in the world. Fortunately, most of our sugar is sold in advance to countries like the Soviet Union, so if the price falls we are not as badly affected as some other sugar-producing countries. But we would be much richer if the price of sugar rose by just a few cents a pound! If people knew the work that went into cutting cane and producing sugar perhaps they would be prepared to pay a little more for it. This would help countries like Cuba that depend so heavily on sugar.

9

"Long hours picking the cocoa pods"

Rajo Ragbir grows cocoa in Pepper Village, Gran Couva in Trinidad. When the pods have been harvested, the beans are removed, cleaned, and exported. Rajo's greatest concern is that the price of cocoa will fall, reducing her earnings.

Most of the people in the village are involved in growing cocoa and coffee. They are similar crops to grow and the way we handle them after they are grown is very similar too. Both grow among banana trees which give them shade, and both take about five years from the time of planting to harvesting.

The cocoa harvest lasts from February to June. The cocoa pods are picked and then split open for the beans to be taken out. The beans are surrounded by a sweet, lemony cream that the children like to eat. You can't eat the beans because they are too bitter. The beans are then laid out on the floor of the drying houses, and as they dry they take on the familiar brown color and begin to smell like cocoa. While they are drying we must constantly turn them over, and the best way we have found to do this is with our feet. Slowly shuffling our feet through the beans makes sure they turn and dry properly. Sometimes this is called "dancing" the cocoa, but it is a slow and laborious dance, and not much fun.

The drying houses are built so that the roof can be rolled off to expose the beans to the sun and quickly rolled back at night or when it rains. We have to get rid of the mice that like to nibble the beans while they are drying, and we have lots of cats for that reason.

When we have finally dried the beans we put them into sacks for the factory where they are cleaned and polished and packed for use in other countries. The beans are mainly used for making chocolate or cocoa powder. Few people who enjoy eating these sweet things can imagine the work that goes into making them. They may taste sweet but the work can be truly bitter. We work long hours picking the cocoa pods and then we have to dry the beans once the pods are opened.

A major problem for us is that the price of cocoa on the world market can fall for reasons we don't even know or understand, and there's nothing we can do about it. Of course, when that happens we earn less money. But lately the price of cocoa

The cocoa pods are picked and split open, and the beans are taken out to be dried.

"Dancing the cocoa;" Rajo helps the beans to dry by turning them with her feet.

tages to living in the country because everyone knows their neighbors and friendships are strong. Then there is the fact that in the country nobody ever has to go without food because there is plenty of fruit like bananas, mangoes and breadfruit, and roots like yams.

has been high so we must take advantage while we can, although there is no way we can grow new trees quickly. By the time our new trees have been planted and the cocoa harvested, the price could have dropped again.

It's not all bad, though. There are advan-

"There's a magic about the area"

Art Hansen is an American who runs a jewelry shop in St. Barthélemy in the French West Indies where he lives for half the year. The other half he spends in Santo Domingo, the capital of the Dominican Republic.

The Caribbean really gets to you! I have lived down here for more than twenty years now and couldn't live anywhere else. It isn't just the sun and the fantastic sea, or even the beauty of the islands. There's a magic about the whole area. But

A *diver searching for precious stones and coins in the wreck of* La Concepcion.

each island has its own character. Everywhere you go, the people are different in many small ways. Just by the way they walk I can tell if a person is Dominican, Puerto Rican, or Cuban.

We could hardly be more different here in the Dominican Republic from our neighbors in Haiti; on the same island but ages apart. There is great poverty in Haiti but nobody has to go hungry in the D.R. There's sugar, rice, cattle, every tropical fruit you can imagine, and the sea around the coast teems with fish and shrimp. The people here are industrious, too, and some of the friendliest people in the area. I should know – I married one of them!

There are other things here besides agricultural riches. The D.R. is famous for its amber and other precious stones. Amber is formed from fossilized pine resin which can be millions of years old. The people in the east of the country dig up the soil, sifting it like gold prospectors. Then when they find the amber it has to be cut and finished. The most rare and expensive pieces contain insects which were caught in the resin as it set. Scorpions are the most sought after but ants and wood borers are common and not very expensive.

There are other precious stones and valuables to be dug out of the ground, or from the seabed. The pendant I wear around my neck came from the bottom of the sea. It is a silver piece of eight from the Spanish ship *La Concepcion*, which went down off the coast of the D.R. in 1641, loaded with treasure. After fifteen years of diving, and research in London and Spain, its position was pinpointed by an American, Burt Webber, who recovered all the treasure – gold and silver worth 27 million dollars. Half of that money went to the Dominican Republic government and the rest to the American investors who paid for the recovery. We also know the position of three other ships off the coast which could be recovered, and I might just get involved in bringing up the next one. Before I die I'd like to sail a midget submarine, and this would give me the chance. But I know how treacherous the Caribbean Sea is. You can never take it for granted because it can change from being calm one minute to stormy the next. But most of my life has been spent near the Caribbean and I don't think I'll ever be too far away.

Amber pendants on display in a store in Santo Domingo.

"Here, the big fish eat the little fish"

Tony Jackson is 18 years old and lives in the Cité Simon area of Port-au-Prince, the capital of Haiti. He is unemployed but tries to make a living by showing foreign tourists around Haiti.

I am eighteen years old and I have never worked in my life. There are many people like me in Haiti. We have to do the best we can and life can be very hard. There are ways of getting a job: if you have a friend in the army, for example, he can look after you. He can say, "I know this man, he is my friend. Give him a job." But that is really the only way. Here, the big fish eat the little fish.

So I try to make a living, if you can call it that, by being helpful to people who come to visit Haiti. For example, some German tourists wanted to visit the Citadel at Cap-Haïtien, so I helped make all the arrangements for the trip and made sure everything went smoothly for them.

Paintings and vegetables on sale in a street in Port-au-Prince, Haiti.

Tony tries to make a living showing tourists around Haiti.

I even made sure that nobody else would bother them. So they paid me for helping them and even sent me a shirt from Germany when they got back home. Working like that, helping people as a guide, is the only way I can survive because everything in Haiti costs so much.

Housing is incredibly expensive here: $80 a month just to rent a room. But for that much money a whole family can feed itself and, as you can imagine, eating comes before anything else. That is why you find so many people here living in really awful conditions. Some people make their own houses, if you can call them that, out of whatever they can find – cardboard, sheets of plastic, anything. You cannot imagine the conditions in which some people live in Port-au-Prince. In Cité Simon, where I live, the conditions are the worst you will find anywhere. The houses look as if they will blow away: water and sewage run down the middle of the street. It is very unhealthy there and many people get ill, but there is nothing they can do about it. The people seem to have given up. Many of them are starving, and their children, too.

That is why so many people go to church to pray. It is the only thing they can do. They cannot work, they cannot eat, they have nowhere to go. The only thing left to do is to pray to God that things will change. The Pope came to Haiti in 1983, to the Cathedral in Port-au-Prince, and everyone hoped there would be a miracle, but we are still waiting for it.

I have no education because I have never been to school. There are few schools here and even at the church schools you have to pay. Few can afford the fee although it isn't very much. I can speak a few languages and I practice whenever I get the chance, so that I can speak to people who come to visit, but they seem to be getting fewer and fewer. I have to force myself not to give up hope.

"The ferry is a vital link"

Arthur Anslyn lives in Charlestown on Nevis. He has been a seaman all his working life, and now captains the ferry that runs between Nevis and its sister island, St. Kitts, about 3 kilometers (2 miles) away.

The two islands of St. Kitts and Nevis are less than 3 kilometers (2 miles) apart, but for some people living here they could be on opposite sides of the world. There are still people who have never visited their sister island and have no need, or desire, to do so.

Part of Basseterre, the largest town on the island of St. Kitts.

The ferry is a vital link even though it only runs twice a day; from Nevis to St. Kitts and back again, first thing in the morning, and then a second journey in the late afternoon. It means that people can go to work on the different islands, or just visit their friends and relatives. The ferry is also the main communication link between Nevis and the outside world because we carry the mail. And, of course, we also carry important and urgently needed goods and spare parts between the islands.

The people here depend on the ferry and there has to be a good reason for it not to run. In the past we've had various boats that were reliable after a fashion, but the one we have now is fast and dependable. The trip only lasts a few minutes; in the past it was a long, slow haul, with boats rarely leaving on time. Things are a bit better organized now, but then the Caribbean as a whole is a bit better organized. We are developing, perhaps not as fast as we would like, but slowly

The Caribe Queen *ferrying passengers between Nevis and St. Kitts.*

and surely we are getting there, and largely under our own steam. The other countries of the world don't have a monopoly on expertise and talent: there's a lot of it here in the Caribbean. It has always been here. It's just that now there is more opportunity for it to come out. Better education helps: it means that the talent we have doesn't stay hidden. Of course, when there are economic difficulties in the rest of the world we tend to be affected even here in the Caribbean. It's often said that if the developed part of the world sneezes we catch a cold, and that is probably true.

But look around any of the islands and you will see we are moving forward. The people have a better living, the children are better cared for and are getting a good education. There are better opportunities for everybody.

Me, I'm happy as the skipper of this ferry. I've always been at sea traveling between the islands, and it's too late for me to change now. Anyhow, I don't want to change. I'm happy doing what I've always done and doing it well.

"We never take the sea for granted"

Cecil Murray is a 26-year-old lifeguard at Stone Bay, Crown Point, on the island of Tobago. He patrols the beach to try to prevent swimmers from getting into trouble, and to rescue them if they do.

A lot of people envy me my job. I can swim every day in the clearest water from one of the best beaches on Tobago. I keep in shape, I work in the open air and I get to meet people from all over the world. And I get paid for it.

But my job is a responsible one which I, and all the other lifeguards, take very seriously because if we didn't, people's lives would be in danger. We work here every day of the week, patroling the beach area and keeping a lookout from our tower. We mark out the beach with flags to indicate the areas safe for swimming. When on patrol we carry our rescue "can" – a kind of float. If bathers get into difficulties we are able to keep up to seven people afloat on the one "can." The secret, however, is not to let anyone get into trouble. By patroling the beach we can point out to families the dangers of inflatable rafts and kick boards. We can point out the

Flags are used to mark the areas of the beach where it is safe to swim.

Cecil patrols the beach at Stone Bay, with his rescue "can" over his shoulder.

rocky areas and keep people away from them as well as be aware, ourselves, of the dangers of tides at particular times of the year.

Holidays and weekends are the most difficult and busy times for us and we may even have guards in the water as a precaution. We can never take the sea for granted. Since we were established in 1976 there has never been a death by drowning at our beach. Swimmers have been in trouble but we've always been able to rescue them and give them attention before sending them to a hospital. All the lifeguards are trained as paramedics, and have skills such as resuscitation, which can mean the difference between life and death for someone in trouble. We are never satisfied though, and are always looking for better equipment and better ways of doing our job.

We have a reputation for being playboys because we have such a pleasant job — some would even call it glamorous. But all the glamor goes when we have to get out to sea fast, bring back a victim and get him or her breathing again. That's a lot of responsibility and no amount of looking good on the beach will make up for not being able to handle that situation when it arises.

"All the children are in danger"

Betty Macintosh is a Baptist missionary from Canada, working at Kemscoff in the mountains of Haiti. The mission there runs agricultural programs to help the local farmers, educational projects, and a hospital.

The first missionaries who came here were working for the spiritual salvation of the people, but they soon realized that in the midst of such misery and poverty it was necessary to concentrate on other things. So missionaries began to develop agricultural programs to help people who were literally starving. Water is a big problem here, too, so systems of terracing were started which helped to conserve the water and make agriculture more feasible. Plants were developed that were suited to the climate, would grow easily, and give a good yield. All these things are, of course, in addition to our missionary and educational work.

From small beginnings, over forty years ago, we now have more than 200 churches in Haiti, and as many schools. Since our intention is that Haitians will eventually take responsibility for everything we have set up, all our pastors are Haitians and so are as many of the teachers as possible. In the hospital we run at the mission all the staff are Haitian.

Terracing the fields makes it more feasible to grow crops on the mountainside.

The mission at Kemscoff performs a number of functions. We have a self-help agricultural project where we enter into agreements with local farmers. We provide them with seed and then buy the produce from them, selling it in the mission store. We also grow our own ornamental plants to help pay for our medical service.

The hospital runs an outpatients department, and we have a men's ward, a women's ward, and one for children. Tuberculosis is common in Haiti because of the rainy season. The people don't have dry clothes and their wood becomes too wet for them to burn for warmth or to cook food on. This is a real problem so we have an infectious diseases ward for tuberculosis and other diseases.

When the first missionaries came here during the 1930s all the hills were covered with pine forests. They have almost all been cut down to make charcoal as a fuel for cooking. The absence of trees has meant that the soil has been eroded away by the rain. We are trying to contribute to the reforestation of Haiti by giving farmers small trees to plant to replace those that have been lost. We have had some success in this and the new forests have virtually all come from our project.

We consider our educational programs very important for children of nursery age right through to adults. For preschool-age children we have a project – "Headstart" we call it – which involves health care and food, as well as education. The children are given a high protein meal with all the vitamins they need. All the children are in danger: almost 50 percent of them die before they reach five years old, so we must do something.

There is terrible poverty and hardship here and we can only hope that our work will help to end it. It is a difficult job but we continue to work and pray that it will succeed.

The mission grows and sells ornamental plants to help pay for its medical service.

"Our blend is a very special secret"

Owen Tulloch is the Chief Blender for Appleton's Rum, which is produced by Wray and Nephew in Kingston, Jamaica. To arrive at the correct blend he relies upon his keen sense of smell and years of experience.

The Appleton Estates are in the southwest of Jamaica, surrounded by the cane fields which give us our sugar and our rums. Here in Kingston we take on the job of aging, blending, and bottling the rum as well as producing various kinds of wine and liquor under license. My nose is important for insuring that the blending of our rums is correct.

The manufacture of rum is very similar to that of Scotch whisky. Rums of different years that have been aged in wooden casks are blended together to make our own very special taste. Once a rum is distilled it is aged in a cask made from American white oak that has previously held whisky. The casks come to us broken down and our coopers build up the barrels again — a very traditional craft. One of our major problems, once we have put the rum in the barrels for aging, is loss through evaporation. We must keep the warehouses where

This old still was used by Wray and Nephew for distilling rum.

the barrels are stored as cool as possible
and, since air conditioning would be far
too expensive, we flood the roofs with
water to keep the temperature down.

Our company has been in existence for
more than 160 years now, and when President Reagan came to visit our island we
were able to present him with a case of
our 100-year-old rum. That is not a rum
that we normally market. Our 15-year-old
rum is considered as good as the very best
cognac and we sell that to between forty
and fifty countries around the world.

The founder of our company, John
Wray, blended his own rums behind the
counter of the Shakespeare Tavern in the
center of Kingston. He was so successful
that he took his nephew Charles Ward into
the business and moved to larger premises
near the docks. This was more convenient
since the rum was brought into Kingston
by ship. But that wasn't the only reason
they set up shop there — it was also the
commercial area of Kingston. The business grew stronger and stronger and
estates were bought to provide the raw
materials for making rum.

Rum is nothing more than molasses to
which water is added and the mixture is
then distilled off at different levels. The
secret is in the distilling and the particular
flavor that each distillery gives to its own
rum. The way we blend our rums is a
special secret that very few people in this
company know. Naturally, we are always
looking for subtle ways to improve the
product, and that is the great advantage
that we have over other rum makers: our
rums are the product of many years of
experience in improving their quality.

"Men and women have equal roles"

Ofelia Sanchez, 21, spends most of her time studying to be a teacher in Matanzas, Cuba. But, for a few weeks each year, she trains as a member of the People's Militia.

I am proud to carry a gun to defend my country. If you look at our history, especially recent history, you will see that we have suffered invasion and attack from outside on many occasions. The danger is not only still there: it is even more acute.

Women play an important part in the armed forces in Cuba.

That is why the whole country is now under arms in the People's Militia. If anyone should be rash enough to try to invade us they will find us defending our homeland to the end. "Homeland or Death" is a rallying cry of our people and it says exactly what we feel.

To see the People's Militia is to see something very impressive. Men and

Members of the Cuban People's Militia are trained in the use of weapons.

women, young and old, have come forward in answer to the appeal from Fidel Castro, our Commander-in-Chief. They have bought their own uniforms — for some people that was no small sacrifice — and given up their free time on weekends to train. All members of the People's Militia are volunteers like myself.

I spend most of my time studying to be a biology teacher, but for a few weeks of the year I come out here to train. I have learned a great deal about methods and tactics of defense and attack, lessons which I could put to good use if the need ever arose. The course here has consisted of weapons training, much of which I already knew about from previous maneuvers, but I have also learned new techniques, such as mine-laying. All the time we are on the course in the field there are explosions going off all around us to get

us used to the noises of war. Without that, the noise would be a terrible shock if we did have to go into combat.

There are many women in the People's Militia. This should not surprise you, since a hundred years ago women fought alongside men against the Spaniards who then ruled our country, and we have continued to play an important part in the armed forces.

The changing role of women in our country has been something of a revolution within the Revolution. In the last twenty-five years, women have become educated and skilled and are now taking on important social, economic, cultural, and political positions in the country. More women go to work; more women have important functions in the country. Men and women have an equal role in the household, too. Any man that I marry will need to have the new attitude toward women and not just see me as someone who irons his shirts.

"We must pay to go to school"

Pacho Brito, 17, lives in Santo Domingo, the capital of the Dominican Republic. He goes to school for half of the day and spends the rest of the time earning money by selling fruit in the street.

Going to school in the Dominican Republic doesn't mean spending the whole day in school: it is either a morning or an afternoon. There are not enough schools to go

One of the "kitchens" that sell hot food to the workers in the docks nearby.

around so we have to have shifts. The schools are small and the classes packed full. We don't have much equipment, but that is all we have so we make the best of what little there is.

We all have to buy our own books and paper for school, and sometimes I can't afford them. But I can always borrow from a friend. We all do that – it's the only way we can get through school. If we didn't help each other we could never complete our education, and we must do that if we are going to get anywhere in life.

Besides buying the books and paper, we also have to pay to go to school here. My family is large and my parents are not very well-off, so I work to help out. Lots of students have jobs when they are not in school; mine is selling fruit in the street. It helps to pay for my education and gives me and my family some extra money. Selling fruit is good because here very few people eat sweet things like cakes; they prefer fruit and we have almost every kind of fruit growing here.

Selling in the streets here in Santo Domingo can be a hard life but it can be fun too. Everybody knows me wherever I go. There are some people who always buy from me and I can keep some especially good fruit for them. On the streets you can buy every kind of fruit and vegetable, and even cooked meals. By the docks there are rows of "kitchens," with people cooking meals for the dockworkers or for people passing by. The food is good: you can buy hot and spicy meals for just a few pesos. Some people depend on that food being there: they would go hungry without it.

Saturdays and Sundays are good days because then people dress up in their best clothes and walk along by the sea. They usually stop to eat something – some fruit from me or perhaps a meal. Walking past all those "kitchens" makes them very hungry. I know – it makes me hungry too.

Nobody gets rich selling things in the street but it suits me fine because I can earn some extra money. I'm not going to be doing this all my life. I'll keep on studying and when I finish I could be an engineer or go to work for one of the big companies here. I might even be able to travel. I'm sure I will be able to get a good job because the Dominican Republic is growing now. It's really taking off and young people have a good future.

Pacho wheels his cart along the street in Santo Domingo.

"Demand for oil is very low"

Joe Fernandez, 32, is Marketing and Production Manager for West Indies Oil in Antigua. The refinery has closed down because of a fall in the demand for oil, and the storage tanks now hold refined oil from Trinidad and liquid propane from the United States.

We don't have our own oil here although there is always talk about the possibility of oil being found offshore of Antigua. Even if it were there it would be difficult to exploit it at the moment when the world-wide conditions are not good for petroleum.

That is why our refinery is closed down at the moment. Demand for oil all over the world is very low, and even bigger, more developed countries than Antigua

These tanks are used for storing liquid propane imported from the United States.

One of the refinery's storage tanks gets a fresh coat of paint.

have had to close down their refineries. So now we use the storage facilities for refined oil from Trinidad, which is pumped to our containers from an offshore platform, and for liquid propane from the United States.

Our refinery is a relatively small one, refining twenty thousand barrels of crude oil a day when working. When we are in business we work twenty-four hours a day. We can refine crude oil from any part of the world but when we were operating we obtained our oil from Mexico. There are oil deposits in the Caribbean – in Trinidad, Barbados, and Curaçao, and refineries in these countries too. Venezuela has oil, of course, but although its coastline is in the Caribbean we don't think of it as a Caribbean country. If conditions improved we would restart the refinery but it would take us four to six months to start production again.

Unfortunately the plant has been closed down a number of times since it was built. That means there is less work for the Antiguan people who would work here. However, there are still jobs since we are importing and selling refined oil from Trinidad. But it is not the same thing just selling somebody else's products.

There are fewer demands made of me when the plant is not operating and it is important for me to keep fit physically as well as mentally. All sports are very important in the Caribbean, especially cricket. Antigua now has a number of players on the West Indian team. A lot of young people have ambitions themselves to become professionals and there is a lot of talent here. I don't have ambitions like that but I do play a lot of squash to keep fit, and I jog as well. I don't feel well unless I am physically fit.

"The National Forest is a protected area"

Carmen Gajate is a forest ranger in the Caribbean National Forest near Fajardo, Puerto Rico. The cool climate of the forest region makes it popular with visitors from nearby San Juan, and its heavy rainfall provides water for other parts of the country.

Before Christopher Columbus came to the Caribbean, nearly five hundred years ago, the whole of Puerto Rico was like the Caribbean National Forest today. Now only 3 percent of the country is untouched natural forest and there are constant threats to the land and its wildlife that must be checked. Man has a terrible record when it comes to spoiling the natural beauty of the Caribbean, and especially here in Puerto Rico. The National Forest is a specially protected area, but this doesn't mean it is completely safe: a carelessly thrown cigarette or match could do untold damage.

The rain forests of Puerto Rico are important not only as the sole remaining area of natural vegetation, but because of the rain that falls there. Even when the rest of the country suffers a drought there is usually some rainfall here, which means the plants can grow, the animals that live

The National Forest is very popular with visitors from the capital, San Juan.

A view over the National Forest towards Fajardo and the sea.

here can survive, and the people of Puerto Rico get supplies of water.

There are still some people living in the forest who were here before it was designated a protected area. They have a good life: they pay no rent or taxes and can collect most of their food just by digging it up or picking it off the trees. But the most famous inhabitant of the National Forest is the symbol of Puerto Rico, *coqui*, a little gray-green tree frog that has always been here.

The frogs are called *coqui* because that is exactly the noise they make at nightfall. It is said that *coqui* can only live in the forest and would die of a broken heart if taken out. That may be right because I have never heard of *coqui* living anywhere else.

During the hot times of the year, especially during the spring when there is no rain, the people of Puerto Rico like to visit the rain forests because of the coolness of the climate. There are three million people in Puerto Rico – more than half a million of them in the capital, San Juan – and I'm sure they all come to the forest at some time. It's terribly hot and dry in the city but up here it is always fresh and cool because we are much higher. There is certainly no need for airconditioning. The air is healthy and everyone goes away feeling better for their visit. Those of us who can work here, taking care of the forest, are very fortunate, being able to spend so much time in the mountains.

"Making a cigar is a work of art"

Gilbert Cuff, 54, is the head cigar roller at the Jamaican Tobacco Company's factory in Kingston, Jamaica. He has worked there for over 38 years and now teaches other employees the art of cigar making.

I left school at fifteen and a half and I have worked for the Jamaican Tobacco Company ever since. I took a vacation job and enjoyed it so much here that I never went back to school. I started right at the bottom of the ladder but I am now head cigar roller and trainer, with some two hundred people to supervise.

Most of the workers in our cigar factory are women and that is probably true in other cigar factories. The job is good for women because the hours are flexible which means they can fit in the work here with other responsibilities, and many women bring up a family without a man. Perhaps women are more dexterous than men because once they have learned the art of cigar rolling they just seem to get better and better at it. As the work here is piece work – which means they are paid for what they produce – the faster they work the more they get paid.

We make cigars here for export all over the world. Many people are switching to Jamaican cigars because they are milder

Gilbert is putting the finishing touches to a large cigar.

and sweeter than Cuban cigars. Cuba has always been the most famous country for cigars, and it still is, but we are giving them a run for their money now.

Making a cigar is a work of art – like making a sculpture – so much so that it is almost a pity for it to go up in smoke. The filler – the tobacco that makes up the main body of the cigar – is carefully selected, and when rolled it must have exactly the right consistency. If it is too tight, or not tight enough, then the cigar does not smoke correctly. The wrappers must be perfect as well, with every leaf complete, of the right texture and color, and, from our point of view, it must be neither too damp nor too dry. Our graders are very skilled in selecting the best leaves so we can make what we think are the best cigars anywhere. The climate here is just right for growing tobacco. We have sunshine all year round and the right amount of rain, and the soil is good. Having said that, tobacco is a sensitive plant and has to be handled very gently. Here in Jamaica, the families who grow tobacco have done so for generations, and they know all the tricks of growing the leaves just as we need them and our customers enjoy them.

A grader sorts through tobacco leaves to be used for making cigars.

"Jamaica is the roots of Rasta"

Jahbo Akiso, 26, makes sandals and other leather goods at Olga's Sandals Shop in Basseterre on the island of St. Kitts. He is a Rastafarian and, as such, eats only vegetables and no meat or fish.

Most people don't understand what Rastafarianism is all about. I didn't either until 1974 when I became a Rasta and got to know a little more about my own culture, the black culture. That's what being

Jahbo makes a new pair of leather shoes.

a Rasta is all about, it is something special for black people. It is the black people's culture.

There are Rastas, now, all over the world. Jamaica is the roots of Rasta but there are Rastas in the United States and Britain. Wherever there are black people you will find Rastas.

We grow our hair, our locks, because it is natural and it is a way of identifying ourselves as Rastas. We only eat vegetables because they are natural too. We don't eat meat because it is unclean to the body. To be a Rasta you must see and feel life to the full and to do that you can live off the land. You don't have to eat meat, or even fish. *Ital* food is what we eat. *Ital* food is food from the earth. That is why Rastas smoke *ganja* – because it comes from the earth. It is *Ital*.

Rastas get along well with all other Rastas, but then we get along well with everybody. We have no disagreements with white people.

The Bible is the Rasta's guide because

A view from the Brimstone Hill Fortress on St. Kitts. Nevis is in the background.

we all have to know right from wrong. We don't have to study – nobody forces us – but as Rastas we must elevate ourselves. We must make something better of ourselves in the way we live and the way we treat other people.

That is one of the reasons why I work for myself. I can develop myself as a craftsman. Whenever I make something out of leather, such as shoes or a bag, I am putting a bit of myself into it. Each time I make something I put more of myself into it because I want to make it better each time. But then work is hard to find in St. Kitts. I think it is like that everywhere. Since I have my own business, I can always find work and I have somewhere to live. My shop is a place for other Rastas to come to, like a meeting place.

One day, perhaps, Rastas will be able to organize themselves to work together more than they do now. Then we will be taken more seriously because we will be a strong force. Already, in different countries, Rastas are setting up their own businesses and working together. That must be the way forward for black people everywhere, not just in the Caribbean.

"The best of everything for our guests"

Gillian Gutteridge lives on Tortola in the Virgin Islands, but spends most of her time in Antigua, where she and her husband own the Copper and Lumber Store Hotel at Nelson's Dockyard, English Harbour. She is English but has lived in the Caribbean for 12 years.

Although we are English we think of ourselves as Caribbean now. My husband Gordon has lived here for twenty-seven years and I have been here for twelve. Our home is on Tortola but we spend most of the year in Antigua, commuting by plane. Planes are the best way of getting around – not as picturesque as yachts, but more efficient.

The Copper and Lumber Store Hotel belongs to us, and so do some of the other buildings here. Nelson's Dockyard was a ruin until the 1950s when money was raised, much of it in London, to begin its restoration. We have made a small contribution to its restoration by running the hotel. At the same time, I think we are bringing work to Antigua and helping to make English Harbour a splendid working dockyard.

We have very strong views about how the hotel should be run. We were determined that it should be an "up-scale" hotel, providing the best of everything for our guests. Then we have tried to recapture the spirit of the eighteenth century, when the dockyard was at its height. So, I have carefully recreated the furnishings of the period, and each room is authentically decorated and furnished. We have

Antigua is very popular with sailing enthusiasts from many parts of the world.

English Harbour is protected from storms by the hills which almost surround it.

an agent in Britain looking for antiques for us, like the ship's chests we have in each room. The rooms take their names from the ships in Admiral Nelson's fleet. We think we offer a very special something to our visitors: we can't take them back to the eighteenth century but we can give them a taste of it. Of course, they have to pay for the privilege.

The hotel operates throughout the year, although the "season" proper only lasts from December to the end of April when the Antiguan Regatta is over. During the Regatta, Nelson's Dockyard really comes to life, with boats jamming the harbor and over three thousand people here.

Antigua has become our second home. The people here are industrious and friendly and there are none of the tensions found in some of the other islands. We were encouraged to set up the hotel by people already living here, and since we've been here we've not had a moment to think; there has been so much to do. There are said to be ghosts of Nelson's men here but if they have appeared we have been too busy to notice them.

"We spend a lot on health"

Julian Romero Perez drives an ambulance for the Red Cross at the Cacivto Garcia Hospital in Havana, the capital of Cuba. In his spare time he earns extra money taking pictures of tourists on an old instant camera.

The camera I use to take photos is very old, but I think that is why people like me to take their photos. The camera was made in the U.S. in the 1930s and has had a lot of use since then. But it still works well. The process is like that used for the first photographs taken in France over a hundred years ago, except that I produce the photos in just five minutes inside the camera itself.

Taking photos earns me a bit of extra

Julian develops an "instant" photograph inside his camera.

The city of Havana and, in the distance, the start of a violent storm.

money – and we can all do with some of that. In the past, Cuba has been short of many goods – especially consumer goods like refrigerators, TVs, and even combs! In those days, money didn't have much value, but now the stores are full of all the food, clothes, and machines we can buy, so any extra money helps. Lots of people have part-time jobs to help out, and a car mechanic or someone with skills can earn a lot of money. I usually bring out my camera on weekends or holidays, when people are not at work and might like to have a photograph as a souvenir. Now we have foreign tourists again, mainly from Canada, Europe, and Latin America, and many of them like to have a picture of themselves in Havana.

The rest of the week I drive an ambulance for the Red Cross. This is an important job and one I get great satisfaction from. It's probably the best job I have ever had. We take people to the hospital if they are emergency cases or too ill to get there any other way. When there are accidents we have to get there as quickly as we can.

Fortunately the roads in Cuba, even here in Havana, are not very crowded, so when we do have to drive fast it is not too dangerous.

Health is very important here. I've never been to other places in the Caribbean but I read that the situation is bad almost everywhere else. It was like that here 30 years ago. You could not imagine the problems of disease and people going hungry all the time. Now all that has changed. We have drivers and hospitals even in the most remote areas, and all the doctors and nurses we need. We even send our doctors and nurses around the world, to Africa, Latin America, and to other Caribbean islands. Perhaps in the future we will export our experts instead of our sugar as we do now. Who knows?

The hospital I work in is not new but it is one of the busiest in Havana. Just recently we opened a new hospital which has some of the most modern medical technology in it. We spend a lot on health here, and on education: they are both very important. We have a saying that there is nothing more important than a child. That may be right but I would say that there is nothing more important than a life. That's where my work comes in.

"The people on the ships are well-off"

Juan Antonio Rodriguez is a taxi driver in San Juan, Puerto Rico. He depends for his living on the tourists who visit the island, including those from the cruise ships that dock there.

Taxi drivers are a strange breed. We are, perhaps, the most independent group of people and probably always will be. That is because we work for ourselves and struggle against whatever rules and regulations are set to control us. Everyone thinks taxi drivers earn great amounts of money, and possibly some do, but for most of us it is a hard grind. We must work long hours just to make a living, and the larger a taxi driver's family, the longer hours he has to work. Then there is the problem that we can never depend on making a living. Some days, there is just no demand for taxis and there's little for us to do other than play cards at the side of the street, hoping our luck will change.

We are probably luckier in San Juan than in many other cities because of the cruise ships that dock here. The people on the ships are usually pretty well-off, and are restless having been shut up on board ship for a few days. Even though they have a fantastic time on the ships, they want to enjoy themselves when they

Juan waits for his next fare at one of the city's taxi ranks.

come ashore. Some people want a tour of the city, and Old San Juan, which is restored to how it was hundreds of years ago, is a really beautiful sight. Others want to get as far away from the sea as they can, into the interior to explore the countryside. For a group of people from the ships it isn't expensive to hire a taxi, and they get all the information and local knowledge of the driver thrown in as well.

We are lucky in that most tourists on the cruise ships are American and used to giving good tips. Believe me, we depend on those tips for our living and I don't know what we would do without them. But we can never rely on anything in this line of work, and when the tourist season begins to die all our work dies along with it. Then, all we can think of is how difficult our life is and even talk of getting other jobs. But it is only talk because we enjoy the work, even though we must be a little crazy to do it. When the fares are here we do pretty well, but talk to us when they are not and you would think the world was falling in on us.

Rush-hour traffic on one of the major roads out of San Juan.

"We're small but we're on the map"

Daniel Warren-Kidd is the Headmaster at Warren Hall High School in Kingston, Jamaica. The school, which was founded by Daniel's father, is independent of Jamaica's state education system.

This is a family school which was founded by my father. He wanted to help the poor, to give them the education they didn't have. He even went to prison because of debts incurred by the school and was only freed when Alexander Bustamante, who later became Prime Minister of Jamaica, paid off all the debts. My father has some fame in Jamaica because when Queen Elizabeth came here in 1953 he put his coat over a puddle so she wouldn't get her shoes muddy.

We are an independent school – independent, that is, of the state system of education. We receive no support from the Government so we depend upon tuitions paid by our students. That can be a problem for many families, and when students can't afford to enrol the school suffers. We do give scholarships if there is a need, and of course the need is always there.

This is a small school but we have 250 students in the daytime from 8:00 a.m. to 2:30 p.m., then another shift from 5:30 p.m. to 8:00 p.m. for students who work but want to catch up on their learning. There are just six full-time teachers and four part-time, but we manage well with what we have and get good examination results.

In Jamaica there is an "eleven-plus" exam, the Common Entrance Examination, which takes the "cream of the crop" into the state schools. Those who are left filter into independent schools like this one. That means that we are working with students who, for one reason or another, are not well prepared. Some are completely lost because they have missed out on their basic education before coming here. Nonetheless, we get good results and most of our students go away with some qualifications.

Religion plays an important part in this school and every day begins and ends with a short religious service. But then religion is an important part of Jamaican life. Most people are religious and superstitious at the same time. Many a person may not go to work because of a dream he or she had the night before, and most people's daily chores are set around religious beliefs.

Discipline is important here because we have so many students in such a small space. They are all very fit and healthy; in fact, some of them are almost too fit and healthy and can be a bit unruly, but we don't have any real problems.

There is a lot of satisfaction in making a contribution to Jamaican education, especially as many of our past students now have good jobs. We've done well in sports: for three years running we were Schools Soccer Champions, and we even represented Jamaica in Venezuela at a track and field meet. We're small, but we're on the map.

Daniel takes a class of daytime students for English.

(Above) *These Warren Hall High School students are studying for forthcoming events.*

"A great melting pot of cultures"

Sahadeo Basdeo is a member of the Senate of Trinidad and Tobago, and a lecturer at the University of the West Indies. He is 38 and lives at Chaguanas, Trinidad.

Like most of the Caribbean states, Trinidad and Tobago must develop a new society from the relics of the past. That is why it is necessary for all Trinidadians and Tobagans to understand their history and see it as a guide to what must be done to shape a new society. We were a British colony until 1962, and we still possess much that was left here by the British, including our system of government, although we have modified it somewhat. I'm not sure that the system always works so well in Britain, so I have doubts about its appropriateness here.

We were totally reliant on Britain before independence, but since then we have moved much closer to the United States, which has taken up the role Britain once had in the Caribbean. Perhaps we are now even more dependent upon the United States than we ever were on Britain.

Sahadeo shops for vegetables in the market at Chaguanas.

There is only one hope for Trinidad and Tobago and all the other Caribbean states: we have to achieve some form of unity. There are differences of opinion between many of the states, which make co-operation difficult now or even in the next ten years, but unity will certainly come within the next one or two generations. We must recognize all our differences – in size and power, and our political differences – and face up to them to arrive at a solution which will suit all our communities.

The Caribbean is a great melting pot of many cultures. Not only were the British here, but the French, the Danes, the Spanish, and the Dutch. Then there were the people who came from Africa and India and, in more recent times, the North American influence. Yet there is a common Caribbean culture, and a sense of being part of the region which unites us all. In the long run, that will emerge as being more important than our differences. The new generation of Caribbean people feel that, and they are beginning to act upon it. They are not advocating revolutionary solutions but demanding that their roots, their history, and their status as Caribbean people not be swept aside by influences from outside. They have traveled, many to the U.S. or Britain, and they have seen that we are just as good as anyone else. Their education has not just come from books: their experiences have shown them that Trinidad and Tobago, or wherever else they may be from, are not as backward as they were led to believe. That is why they are confident about the future. Just as I am.

The Basdeo family spend a relaxing day on one of Trinidad's beaches.

"Our visitors are mostly from the U.S."

Dudley Ellis works at the Pegasus Hotel in Kingston, Jamaica. He has spent all his working life in the tourist industry, and has been at the Pegasus since it opened in 1973.

Tourism is very important to Jamaica. Before the growth of the bauxite industry, tourism was the third most important industry in the economy. Then sugar and bananas declined and tourism was number two behind bauxite. Now that bauxite is not so important tourism has to be first, and yet we are barely scratching the surface even now. There has been a resurgence of tourism in Jamaica in the 1980s after a fall-off in the 70s. Our visitors are mostly from the U.S., although there are growing numbers from Europe

Drinks by the pool for some of the Pegasus Hotel's guests.

Beaches like this one attract many visitors to Jamaica and other Caribbean islands.

and increasingly from Japan. This hotel, the Pegasus, is not like the tourist complexes along the northern coast where the trade is very seasonal. Our clientele are predominantly business people so we are full almost all the year, just slowing down a bit at Christmas time.

I have worked at the Pegasus since it opened in 1973. It's fascinating to work here because I get to meet so many important people of different nationalities and different cultures. I've always worked in some aspect of tourism and I wouldn't change that for the world.

Everyone in Jamaica now recognizes the importance of tourism to the economy. Talk to anyone in the street and you will find Jamaicans more helpful and polite than they were a few years ago, because everyone now knows that we depend upon tourism for our foreign exchange and, many of us, for our jobs as well. Without my job I would never have been able to educate all my children the way I have. They all have good jobs and a good education but they have a very different outlook from my own. They are aware of all that goes on in the world, and there is no way young people can be taken for granted any more. Some young people have turned away from tourism. They see a job like mine as servile. That's not the case; what we offer here is warm hospitality. It's a rewarding and satisfying occupation because we are working for our country at the same time. Our politeness and courtesy and general attitudes are important because when people come to Jamaica, to our hotel, we want to show them that they really are welcome. By our reception we are saying, "Come again."

"Tourism is a mixed blessing"

Marcilia Nelson, 30, is a lay preacher in the Methodist Church in Barbados. She lives in Christchurch but travels all over the island preaching to church congregations and visiting people in their homes. She also works for the school meal service in Barbados.

Some people have a "calling" to God almost overnight. It wasn't like that with me but I felt the "calling" nonetheless. I used to read the lessons in church, and became very interested in Christianity and got involved in the work of the Church. I felt as if God were leading me to the Church.

I became a lay preacher, and since 1983 I have been traveling throughout the whole of Barbados as a preacher. We have thirty churches, but my work also takes me into the homes of people who, because they are ill or infirm, can't get to church.

Religion used to be central to life in the Caribbean. It is still important for many, giving guidance and leadership, but there are changes occurring because of exposure to different values. Education has contributed to this. Caribbean people travel more too; not much within the Caribbean but to the United States, Canada, and Britain. Then, there are the tourists who come to our islands, bringing with them the examples of different values. Tourism is a mixed blessing for us. I'm not sure that

Marcilia talks to some of the congregation after a church service.

anything has replaced religion because a lot of people still come to church and still believe in God, but there are changes occurring.

The Church has seen the changes and responded to them. We can no longer stand by and ignore the pressing social problems that exist. There is the problem of unemployment which affects all the islands, and many people still don't have running water or decent housing. The future of the Church must be to become more involved in the social areas of life as well as the spiritual. We must work for better human rights because the Church touches every part of life. Or it should.

The work I do makes a real contribution to people's lives. The school meal service in Barbados provides meals for all school children and this has improved the health of the population since the 1950s, when it was introduced. Now we have no malnutrition among the young people and everyone's health is better. Better education as well as better food has also contributed and we must all keep up the pressure to make sure we don't slide back.

One of the thirty Methodist churches on the island of Barbados.

"I could not stand the British climate"

Iteh Brown left his home in the West Indies in the 1960s and moved to London, England. But he missed the Caribbean and soon returned. He now lives at St. Mary's Parish in Antigua and works on a pineapple plantation.

I was one of those people who left the West Indies in the 1960s and went to Britain. I lived in London for a few years and got a good job. I was able to buy things that I could only have dreamed about on Antigua. But, I just could not stand the British climate. The summers weren't warm and the winters were bitter. I was cold no matter how many clothes I put on. Even inside the house I was cold. So I came back home and, although I don't have the money to buy so many things, I feel much happier in my mind.

When I was in London I would look at all those people from the West Indies and to me they always looked out of place. They never seemed to look happy, but perhaps that was because I wasn't happy. I always missed my home and my life in the Caribbean.

I am happy here, working on the land. Working in agriculture is a very satisfying life, even when you are working for someone else as I am. My job is to help with the cultivation of the pineapples on the plantation. We grow a very special pineapple called Black Diamond. It is the sweetest, juiciest pineapple there is, and not hard and woody like some. It has been on the island a long time but, because nobody took the trouble to cultivate it, it almost died out. The government has helped to encourage people to grow it by giving them grants, and has even started up its own plantations.

My work is anything that needs to be

A new crop of Black Diamond pineapples growing in one of the plantation fields.

done on the farm. I might be planting new plants, or helping with fertilizing, weeding, or picking.

You have to know precisely the right moment to cut the fruit. Not too soon, not too late, otherwise it is not at its best. My son helps me sometimes when he is not at school, but gathering the fruit is skilled work; the pineapples are easily bruised and damaged and you must wear gloves to avoid being cut by the spines of the plant.

We have a little land we cultivate for ourselves as well as a few animals, so we never go hungry. I count myself lucky and I thank God for it. It's good to be back home again with my own people.

Pineapples and other fruits on sale at a roadside stall.

"We are using new technology"

Alicia Govia, 19, comes from Port-of-Spain, Trinidad, but is currently studying business administration at the university in San Juan, Puerto Rico. When she graduates she would like to join her parents' construction company.

I am an only child and my family did not want me to study too far from home. But we have friends in Puerto Rico and my parents said they were happy for me to go to live with them and study there. I didn't want to study in my own country but Canada and the U.S. seemed too far away. Also, I thought it would be exciting to learn a new language – the people in Puerto Rico speak Spanish. Spanish has to be the next most important language to English. Just look at the countries of the world where it is spoken – nearly all of Latin America, parts of Africa, Spain, of course; even in the United States there are millions of Spanish-speaking people.

The Prime Minister of Trinidad and Tobago's splendid residence in Port of Spain.

In college, I chose to study business administration, specializing in information systems. This was partly because my parents are in the construction industry in Port-of-Spain, and I wanted to study subjects that would give me the potential to contribute something to my family's business. Some people seem to think that we are backward in the Caribbean, and perhaps in some ways we are. But we are using new technology as it comes along, and I wanted to learn something about the information revolution since it will have tremendous implications for all businesses, not only my family's.

But I'm not a student all the time. I like to enjoy myself, as all young people do, and in Trinidad the bonds of friendship are very close. Here, when you make friends you are friends for life. So, for me, Trinidad always comes first. In the past a lot of people in the Caribbean wanted to identify with the U.S. or Canada or Britain, but now many Trinidadians who did go away are returning home to their roots. I think the people of Trinidad are beginning to appreciate what we have here and to make a real effort to get on together.

There are still racial problems among Indians, blacks, whites and others, and we have to try to stop thinking about our differences and come together. The young people mix more these days, which must be a good sign for the future, but the old will never change. They have set ideas about other races. Marriage, in particular, can be a big problem. But if what I want to do is marry a Puerto Rican or an Indian boy, that's what I'll do. It might be hard for my parents but I have my own life to live.

Alicia is a student in the bustling city of San Juan, Puerto Rico.

"People seem to prefer paying a fee"

Errol Walrond is Professor of Surgery at the University of the West Indies, based at the Queen Elizabeth Hospital in Bridgetown, Barbados. He qualified as a doctor in London and returned to the Caribbean in 1965.

Like many doctors in the Caribbean, I studied abroad first of all, at Guy's Hospital in London. I returned in 1965 and taught at the University of the West Indies in Jamaica until 1974 when I came back to my native Barbados.

Unlike some countries, such as Britain and Canada, we have no National Health Service as such. Medical care is in private hands but that doesn't mean that those people who can't afford to pay get no treatment. The Barbados government provides health centers for the old and the very poor, and emergency rooms, like the one in this hospital, are open and available, free, to everyone. There is a plan to implement a system of free health care for the island, but people seem to prefer paying a fee here. They feel that if they are paying then they are getting more from their doctor. People can afford to go to the doctor because fees are not high here.

The kinds of illnesses we have in the Caribbean vary from place to place but the pattern is moving toward that of Europe and North America. Diseases of the developed countries, like diabetes and hypertension, are now our main concerns, and cancer is also a major worry.

Infectious diseases are still a problem, especially in the less developed islands where there might not be a good water supply. But tropical diseases, such as malaria and yellow fever, have almost disappeared. There are a few pockets of malaria in Belize and Guyana, and in Haiti, too, from where exiles fleeing the country have taken the disease to the Bahamas. But that is well under control. Yellow fever, which used to be a killer throughout the Caribbean, has now all but gone. There was a brief scare in Trinidad a few years ago when hunters in the deep forest areas contracted the disease, which is still carried by the monkey population there. But these occurrences are very rare.

The same mosquito that carries yellow fever also carries a fever called dengue, which breaks out from time to time. Usually it is like a very bad "flu," and is often referred to as "break-bone" fever because that's just how you feel.

Most people in the Caribbean are now better off than they were and this has meant improved nutrition and therefore a greater resistance to disease. Education, too, has raised everyone's awareness of diet, hygiene, and the prevention of disease. Young doctors are now very interested in the idea of preventive medicine, which must bode well for the future. The problem is that governments sometimes drag their feet when it comes to cooperating with the health profession. Health should come before politics.

The Queen Elizabeth Hospital in Bridgetown, Barbados.

Professor Walrond and one of his nurses examine a patient's X ray.

"Each island has its own special charm"

Lilia Cadet is a 29-year-old flight attendant with BWIA – British West Indies Airline, "Bee Wee" for short. She lives in Diego Martin in Trinidad but flies all over the Caribbean and to London, New York, and Toronto.

I guess you could call us ambassadors for Trinidad and Tobago as well as for "Bee Wee." We are in the public eye all the time we are in our uniforms – in the air and on the ground. We must always look smart and create a good impression. But let me assure you that there is much, much more to this job than how you look. There is a discipline that must be learned, as well as a knowledge of safety procedures and other skills. If anyone is thinking of coming into this job just for the glamor, they ought to think again.

We are all very aware that we are the representatives of our national airline. Trinidadians and Tobagans expect a lot extra of us for that reason. But that's not the only reason we try to be the best. These days, international air transport is very competitive and we at "Bee Wee" want to be up there with the front runners, so we try to offer our customers something extra. We call it our Caribbean hospitality. It is not really something we have to work at because in the Caribbean we are famous for our warmth and hospitality.

Sometimes it can be hard for us to know exactly where our home is because of our work. We fly throughout the whole Caribbean, and although we rarely have stopovers on Caribbean flights we do take the opportunities offered to visit the different islands. Each one has its own atmosphere

Passengers boarding a BWIA jet bound for New York.

A BWIA Tri-star takes off from Coolidge airport, Antigua.

and special charm. Puerto Rico has a lovely old city, San Juan, and is wonderful for shopping, as well as having good beaches and peaceful spots in the country. Barbados is very geared up for having visitors and the people are famous for their friendliness. The small islands like St. Kitt's, Nevis, and Antigua are more restful for short stays. But then I think Tobago is very hard to beat; you can relax on beautiful, deserted beaches and just let yourself unwind under the sun.

Of course, we also fly to New York, London, and Toronto which could not be more different from the islands. Usually we can stay a few days between flights so we can get to know the place, visit all the sights, and prepare ourselves for the return leg of the flight. You can spend a long time away from home in this job and although it is enjoyable to spend time in some of the most exciting cities of the world, there is nothing quite like coming home. Trinidadian people are very chauvinistic about their country. They know they live in a beautiful land and are proud of what has been achieved. We have a long way to go, but traveling as I do I can see that we are not so far behind some of the richer countries. "Bee Wee" is a good example: we have the latest planes and we give as good service as anyone. Perhaps the Caribbean flavor makes it even better than anyone else's.

Facts

The facts on these pages refer to the states mentioned in the interviews.

Capital cities: Antigua and Barbuda, St. John's (pop. 24,000); Barbados, Bridgetown (17,550); Cuba, Havana (1,924,900); Dominican Republic, Santo Domingo (1,550,700); Haiti, Port-au-Prince (506,500); Jamaica, Kingston (662,500); St. Kitts and Nevis, Basseterre (15,000); Puerto Rico, San Juan (518,700); Trinidad and Tobago, Port of Spain (120,000).

Principal language: English is spoken in Antigua and Barbuda, Barbados, Jamaica, St. Kitts, Nevis, Trinidad, and Tobago. Spanish is the main language in Cuba, the Dominican Republic, and Puerto Rico. In Haiti, French is the official language, but most Haitians speak creole, a mixture of their old native language and French.

Currency: Antigua and Barbuda, and St. Kitts and Nevis use the Eastern Caribbean dollar (EC$) and Puerto Rico uses the US dollar (US$), but the other states have their own currencies – the Barbados dollar (BDS$), the Jamaican dollar (J$), the Trinidad and Tobago dollar (TT$), the Cuban peso, the Dominican Republic dollar (RD$; RD$1 = US$1), and the Haitian gourde (5 gourdes = US$1).

Religion: All islands are predominantly Christian, Antigua, Barbados, Jamaica, St. Kitts and Nevis being mainly Anglican, and Cuba, the Dominican Republic, Puerto Rico, Trinidad and Tobago mainly Roman Catholic. Jamaica also has significant numbers of Hindus, Jews, Muslims, and Rastafarians, and in Haiti the official religion is Roman Catholicism although the folk religion is Voodoo, a cult involving witchcraft.

Population: Antigua and Barbuda 74,000; Barbados 249,000; Cuba 9,700,000; Dominican Republic 5,648,000; Haiti 6,000,000; Jamaica 2,223,400; St. Kitts 35,000; Nevis 9,300; Puerto Rico 3,196,500; Trinidad 1,137,000; Tobago 41,000. All islands have populations consisting mainly of African, European and native Indian stock. Over the centuries, these (and other) races have become very mixed together.

Climate: Tropical. Average temperature between 24°C and 30°C (75°F and 86°F) and rainfall between 125 and 215 cm (50 and 85 ins.) annually. In the mountainous areas, the temperatures are lower and the rainfall higher.

Government: Antigua and Barbuda, Barbados, Jamaica, and Trinidad and Tobago are independent states and members of the British Commonwealth, each having their own Governor-General, nominated or appointed Senate, and elected House of Representatives or House of Assembly. St. Kitts and Nevis is a State in Association with Britain, with the Queen as Head of State, represented by a Governor, and an elected House of Assembly. Cuba is a socialist state with one political party and a government headed by Fidel Castro. The Dominican Republic has an elected President and a Senate and Chamber of Deputies. Haiti is ruled by its President for life, Jean Claude Duvalier, and an elected National Assembly. Puerto Rico, officially the Commonwealth of Puerto Rico, (a self-governing entity in association with the U.S.) is governed by a Senate, House of Representatives, and Governor, all elected.

Housing: Housing is a problem for almost all Caribbean countries. Accommodation varies from high-rise skyscrapers in the capital cities, such as San Juan in Puerto Rico and Havana in Cuba, to tiny dwellings like the *bohio* of Cuba, made from palm and palm thatch. The cities attract a great many people from the surrounding areas because of the jobs and the lifestyle they offer.

Education: On many of the islands, education is free and compulsory up to age of 14, although there are many local variations. In addition, some government-aided and state-owned schools provide free education after 14 – in Barbados and Trinidad and Tobago for example. The states provide most of the educational facilities although there are also private schools in most countries.

Agriculture: Throughout the Caribbean area, the major crop is sugarcane, and it is the most important crop on all of the islands except Haiti, where it is second to coffee. Coffee is also grown in the Dominican Republic, Jamaica, and Puerto Rico. Other important crops are: tobacco, particularly in Cuba, the Dominican Republic and Puerto Rico; cocoa, in the Dominican Republic, Jamaica, and Trinidad and Tobago; and various fruits.

Glossary

Industry: The two major industries in the area are sugar, including molasses and rum, and tourism. Apart from the local production of food and clothing, other industries include chemicals, oil, cement and metals.

Media: Most countries have their own daily newspapers and the larger ones, such as Cuba, the Dominican Republic, Jamaica, and Puerto Rico, have their own radio and TV stations.

Amber   Fossilized resin formed from pine trees which died millions of years ago. It is used as jewelry.

Bauxite   An ore from which aluminum is obtained.

Citadel   A strongly fortified place built to defend a city.

Ganja   Another word, often used by Rastafarians, for marijuana.

Molasses   A thick, brown syrup obtained from sugar during refining.

Paramedic   A person whose work supplements that of the official medical services.

Preventive medicine   Medical care which aims to prolong life by placing a strong emphasis on preventing diseases from occurring, rather than on treating them as and when they appear.

Propane   A gas which is found in petroleum and used as fuel.

Rastafarian   A member of the Jamaican-based religious cult which regards Ras Tafari – the former emperor of Ethiopia, Haile Selassie – as a God.

Regatta   An organized series of races of yachts and other boats.

Rum   A spirit made from sugarcane. It can be colored brownish-red by adding caramel or by leaving it to mature in oak casks, or it can be left colorless.

Tuberculosis   An infectious disease which mainly affects the lungs.

Index